SPICE GIRLS

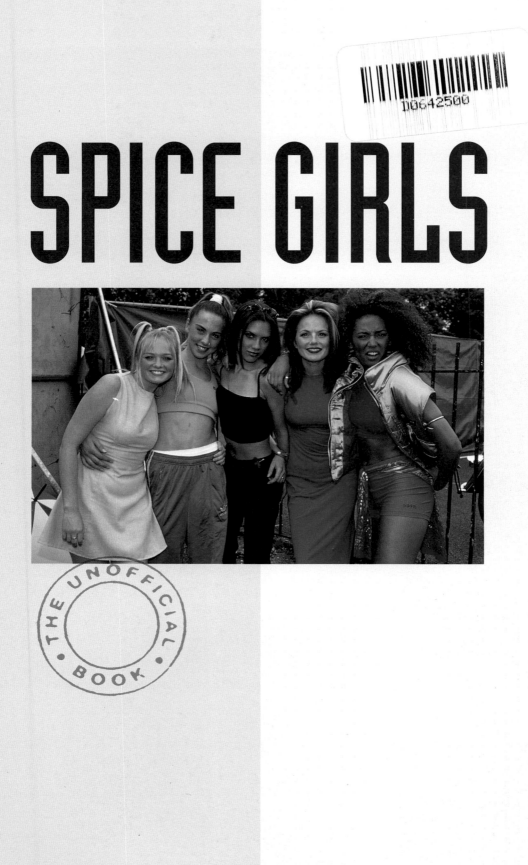

THE UNOFFICIAL BOOK

SPICE GIRLS

THE UNOFFICIAL • BOOK •

THE HOTTEST BAND AROUND

Virgin

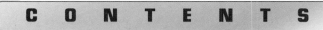

C O N T E N T S

"Boy bands have had their day – it's time to move over." That was the message when Girl Power, in the shape of the Spice Girls, topped the UK charts for the first time in July 1996. 'Wannabe', their first single, written by the five Spice Girls themselves, had an unforgettable catchiness that made it the year's undoubted summer sound. And as a horde of identikit outfits like Let Loose, Upside Down, 911 and Backstreet Boys fought for the throne recently vacated by Take That, the Spices offered a fresh role model for girls to do their own thing, not just watch from the sidelines.

Lads watched and wondered, too, at these five very different characters who seemed to offer something for everyone. Who were they? Where had they sprung from? And what, crucially, was 'zigazig ha'? All these questions and more would soon be answered as Scary Spice, Baby Spice, Posh Spice, Ginger Spice and Sporty Spice took their share of the spotlight. And everyone from The Face to the Daily Telegraph, from Smash Hits to Saturday morning TV, was keen to give them a platform.

Though their individual views differ, the Spice Girls all agree on one thing: they're not a manufactured group. The fact they write their own songs and appear to do just whatever they please, whenever and wherever they want, bears that out.

But like boy band kings Boyzone, who answered an Irish press ad placed by their manager, it did need someone else to bring them together. And though everyone assumed they'd come from out of nowhere to find overnight fame, the Spice Girls' success story was two, nearly three years in the making.

Their story starts with an ad in The Stage, the theatre mag devoured by every Wannabe (oops!) in show business. 'Wanted: Five Girls Who Can Sing And Dance', it read – and guess who applied? What the Girls' new-found Fairy Godfather didn't realise was that the famous fivesome already knew each other. They'd all met on the circuit when attending the endless round of auditions and tryouts every 'overnight success' has to go through as they try to break into showbiz.

Now they were going to take on the rest of the world, together...

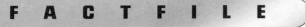

FULL NAME: Melanie Janine Brown

DATE OF BIRTH: 29th May 1975

STAR SIGN: Gemini

PLACE OF BIRTH: Leeds

HEIGHT: 5 ft 5 ins

EYES: Brown

DISTINGUISHING MARKS:
Her huge hair, that pierced tongue, and the tattoo on her tum - a Japanese symbol meaning 'Spirit, Heart and Mind'

WHAT DOES IT TAKE TO MAKE A SPICE GIRL?
Mel B says it's knowing what you want... and wearing lots of blusher!!

IN A PREVIOUS LIFE:
She danced, attended music college (she plays the drums), did tele-sales for a newspaper. And Mel B made a brief appearance in Coronation Street

FIRST CONTACT WITH THE OTHER SPICES:
Met Mel C when they were both performing in a dance troupe

STATED AMBITION:
To have a gold diamond pierced tongue and a monster motorbike

MUSICAL TASTES:
Rap, hip hop and jungle

SPICY SURPRISE:
Mel B's a closet poet, and pens verse about her life

MEL B'S PERFECT MAN SHOULD BE:
Quiet and calm - the complete opposite of her Melness, but not a shy retiring violet. Someone who is spontaneous, has a zest for life and fabulous eyes

DECLARED HUNK IS:
ER's George Clooney

WHAT THE OTHER SPICES SAY ABOUT HER:
She's spontaneous, a great party person, and someone who helps them get out of awkward situations

WHAT HER MUM THINKS ABOUT THE SPICE GIRLS
Mel says she loves everyone in the group, except her!

MEL B SAYS SHE'S THE "FREAK OF NATURE" OF THE GROUP

MELANIE B

In yer face is where Mel B likes to be. A Yorkshire lass, she doesn't beat about the bush, gets straight to the point. She's loud, and proud to be loud. When one photographer dared to suggest she might quieten down a bit, she ripped back "I don't do quiet!!!". A laugh as big as the ocean, and an appetite for life that's larger. She'll try anything once, especially if it might shock people out of their complacency. In fact, she prefers it when people shout back at her - at least that means they're giving her some attention. Her heroes are anyone who challenges conventional rules. She loves having a pierced tongue, but to make sure she knew what it felt like, according to Geri, she insisted that all the other Spices let her snog each of them. Mel C was the first Spice Girl she knew: they shared a bedroom together in their first house and are still always having fights. Move over Liam and Noel. Of course, this means that your average self-conscious wimp of a male is a tad frightened of this self-confessed Northern nutter. No problem: legend persists that Mel B secured her current man by going straight up to him and suggesting he pick her up at 7.30 the next Wednesday night! Funnily enough, though, behind the exterior, she may also be a little bit sensitive... But don't tell her we said so!

EMMA ON MEL B

When Emma first met Mel B she says she thought "You can't say that!", but in time she's realised that, yes, you can, if you don't hurt or harm anyone.

ON BEING THE WAY YOU ARE

Mel B says the Spice Girls aren't perfect, but they don't claim to be more important than other people - they're simply being themselves.

ON ARGUMENTS

According to Mel B, it's mainly her and Mel C who end up having arguments in the band, and it usually ends up in a fight, what she calls real "punch-ups".

ON FRIENDSHIP

Although some of the Spices do have boyfriends, Mel B reckons they don't let men rule their lives. You can't expect boyfriends to last forever, but you can rely on your girlfriends.

ON CHATTING UP THE BACKSTREET BOYS

Mel B reported back that she asked one of the Boys 'Why do you wear sunglasses all the time? You've got beautiful eyes'... And he didn't put them back on again all day!

ON MEN

Because the Spices don't beat about the bush when it comes to having an opinion, some men can find that scary... But if they're what Mel B describes as "cool" and "calm" in themselves, then she knows she can relax and have a great conversation.

ON THE NEW LASS

Another reason that lads are daunted by the New Lass is that they're realising what it was like to be on the receiving end. In Mel B's view, guys have treated lasses like "little girls", and now it's time to fight back.

ON HOW THE SPICES INTERACT

The secret, according to Mel B, is that all five Spices are extremely close and totally, in fact brutally, honest with each other.

ON GETTING YOUR POINT ACROSS

Whatever colour you are, wherever you come from, whether you're overweight or skinny, however you like to dress. Mel B says you should have an opinion and be heard when you want to be heard.

ON ROLE MODELS

Mel B gives Neneh Cherry as an example: when she first came onto the scene, she was an upfront, sexy woman who brought a brand new, totally fresh attitude with her.

ON BOY BANDS

The difference for Mel B is that the Spice Girls can't be easily categorised. She says she was never a fan of any of Take That.

ON WHY SHE'S A VITAL PART OF THE GROUP

Mel B points out her "big" hair, and the fact that every band needs someone in it with big hair.

"I like to shock people.

It makes me laugh.

You can get away with

anything as long as

you're cheeky."

"I feel alive when I do

mad things."

MELANIE JANINE BROWN

When the five Spice Girls to be answered the ad in The Stage, they had in common a gritty determination to succeed in show business – but five more different characters you couldn't have imagined.

Brown-skinned **Melanie Brown** from Leeds had been through music college before coming to London in search of fame and fortune, only to end up selling ads on the phone for newspapers – except when the panto season came around, when she gained employment as a singer or dancer.

Melanie Chisholm had been a teenage Neneh Cherry fan from Widnes in Lancashire before moving south. Thin, slim and well-toned, she tried ballet dancing and session singing before linking up with the others. Women's football was her big passion in life, helping her put hours of aerobics training to good use.

Geri Halliwell hailed from Watford, but had a rather more exotic background with Spanish and Swedish parents. Unlike Mel C who says her school nickname was Holland, because it's flat - she had the kind of shape that gave her the chance to try out as a Page Three girl. A strong exhibitionist streak saw her at the centre of most things Spicy.

Sophisticated, sassy **Victoria Addams** survived the embarrassment of her top falling down on stage in the middle of a dance routine to pursue her showbiz ambitions. She'd also been in another band before the Spice Girls, but was ready and willing to add her favoured wardrobe of designer clothes to the Spice Girls look.

Talented teen **Emma Bunton**, a North London girl, was the smallest and youngest of the quintet. She went to stage school, but the Spice Girls was her first 'proper' job. Her mother was – and still is – a martial arts instructor so, though Emma wears her hair in schoolgirl-style bunches, beware! She can certainly look after herself. And suitably for the girl they call Baby Spice, she'd modelled for a Mothercare catalogue when still a toddler!

All five had rubbed shoulders with fame without making its full acquaintance. Mel B had made a brief appearance in Coronation Street, while Mel C was on the shortlist for the West End stage show Cats: Victoria and Emma had met in a locally-staged musical when they were younger. Geri came across Victoria at a Tank Girl audition, while the two Mels once worked together in a dance troupe. With all their combined abilities, they made a conscious decision that the spotlight would be shared. There would be no one lead singer. Each of the five would get a slice of the action.

Having been 'discovered', the girls were packed off to the London suburbs, where they created the female equivalent of Men Behaving Badly in a small shared flat. It certainly broke down a lot of inhibitions, though you can only guess at the length of the bathroom queue! It was a trial by fire, and after they'd all emerged deciding they quite liked each other, they also concluded they weren't so keen on their management. Extricating themselves from their contractual obligations, they set about doing it their way.

First off was a name – and after writing a song called 'Sugar'n'Spice', it occurred to Geri in the middle of an aerobics lesson (as these things do) that Spice could be a good name. Unfortunately, an American rapper had got there first… but the seed of a good idea had been planted, and soon caught on. Spice Girls they'd be! Next stop was the comparative luxury of a house in Maidstone, Kent: this was a three-bedroom dwelling, with the Mels sharing, Victoria in with Emma and Geri, as the oldest of the group, having her own room.

The next step was to record some of these songs they'd been cooking up and circulate them to potential Spice Daddies looking for the next big thing. And when a demo tape landed on the desk of top manager Simon Fuller he recognised this could be just what he was looking for. Not surprising he should want to represent five feisty women – after all, he managed a world-famous one already: Annie Lennox! Could he do the same for the Spices? Silly question!...

FULL NAME: Victoria Addams

DATE OF BIRTH: 7th April 1975

STAR SIGN: Aries

PLACE OF BIRTH: Hertfordshire

HEIGHT: 5 ft 6 ins

EYES: Brown

DISTINGUISHING MARKS:
Designer clothes, long legs, and a discreet little diamond in her fingernail

WHAT DOES IT TAKE TO MAKE A SPICE GIRL?
Victoria says you need to be happy in yourself

IN A PREVIOUS LIFE:
She was in another band and was a dancer

MUSICAL TASTES:
Anita Baker, Toni Braxton, Sounds of Blackness

SPICY SURPRISE: Victoria revealed that she once flashed to a lift full of people in a US hotel

VICTORIA'S PERFECT MAN SHOULD BE:
A great dresser - when it comes to the opposite sex, she goes for clothes first, shoes second

DECLARED HUNK:
Ray Liotta from Goodfellas, or Jack Dee

WHAT THE OTHER SPICES SAY ABOUT HER:
She's classy, cool, and incredibly organised, plus she's the one they think all the men really fancy

WHAT HER MUM THINKS ABOUT THE SPICE GIRLS
Victoria says when her mum first heard about their antics, she thought her daughter was hanging around with a bunch of hooligans!

VICTORIA

FIRST CONTACT WITH THE OTHER SPICES:
Met Geri in the queue for a Tank Girl audition and knew Emma from a musical they did together when they were little

STATED AMBITION:
To be happy and successful and for all the Spice Girls to remain true to themselves

Miss Addams - Victoria, if you don't mind, never Vicky - puts the class into this class act. A sophisticated lady from Herts who's been breaking hearts wherever she goes. And that's most likely to be Knightsbridge and South Ken when she's not performing or recording, because she's a self-confessed designer label girl whose favourite pastime is shopping. Blessed with long, long legs that can show off clothes to their best effect, Victoria is happiest when she's entering the hallowed halls of Harvey Nichols, Joseph or Gucci. She tackles her shopping with the same organised determination that she brings to everything she does - and which means she's the calm centre of the Spices. Perhaps it's the country setting of the house she shares with her parents, three Yorkshire Terriers and her wonderful wardrobe that provides her tranquil air. Sometimes the others want to crack her cool, collected façade. When the group signed to Virgin, the group plied Victoria (who rarely drinks) with huge quantities of champagne to see if they could get her completely legless. She probably didn't mind: there's a cheeky sense of humour tucked just behind the exterior. Just make sure you never spill red wine all over her favourite suit, and you might just see it.

ON PRE-SPICE AUDITIONS

Victoria describes the Spices as the five who were often turned down for the parts, but found they got on really well. And that's how it all started.

EMMA ON VICTORIA

Emma says Victoria is into "organisation". So if they have an appearance or a commitment at nine o'clock, Victoria's the one up at five to get everything ready.

ON DOING THEIR OWN THING

Victoria pinpoints the fact they write their own material and aren't scared of controversy as a vital part of their attitude. From day one, they said they were going to do what they were going to do.

ON MEN

Apparently, in her pre-Spice life, Victoria got chatted up more often. Now that she's famous, if she's going out locally, then she thinks the men might be a bit scared...

ON CHAT-UP LINES

One approach Victoria remembers is a line one guy tried on after complimenting her on her dress sense, and saying he really liked her clothes. His punchline: "They'd look great on my bedroom floor"!

ON BANDING TOGETHER

Five Spice Girls together would help boost anyone's confidence. Victoria recalls being at some awards party where they saw some bloke she fancied. She says that Mel B's intervention - "My mate fancies you!" might have been embarrassing but it was a real ice-breaker.

ON BOY BANDS AND SCREAMS

Bands like Boyzone, Backstreet Boys and co. have always attracted the screamers, but, thinks Victoria, the Spice Girls are probably the only band really out there for the girls. That's why they get a unique reaction.

ON GARY BARLOW, A CAB RIDE AND GARDENING

This is a story Victoria heard about Gary Barlow. He got into a cab, and there were hundreds of fans pounding on the window, screaming at the top of their voices. Gary, so the story goes, simply turned to the cabbie and said his turnips were doing nicely for that time of year!

ON HER SECRET

Victoria revealed in one interview that she thinks she looks "crap" without any make-up on, and that first thing in the morning, nobody would recognise her. Bet we would.

"Even if nobody liked

us, we'd be doing this

for ourselves.

Having fun and being

successful is a bonus."

VICTORIA ADDAMS

When they were looking for a deal, the great advantage the Spice Girls had over many of their rivals was that they could perform their act anytime, anywhere, acappella (that's unaccompanied to you and me). No record company's office was safe as they led a series of daring, commando-style raids, charming the cheque books out of executives' pockets.

The lucky winners were Virgin Records, founded by Richard Branson, where their labelmates would include... the re-formed Sex Pistols, Meatloaf and Phil Collins! That was just the point: an injection of hot, pure pop sensibility was needed, and Spice Girls were just that. But their launch wasn't hurried, and it would be a year or so before their first release. Before that, there was an album to write and plans to plot – once the five blow-up dolls they brought to the signing session had been retrieved from the River Thames, where they'd been thrown in an excess of enthusiasm!

Their album, to be called simply 'Spice', was written in the studio with two different production teams. Matt Rowe, one half of the Stannard and Rowe duo who co-wrote 'Wannabe' with the girls, claimed the prospect of working with five women for 24 hours a day wasn't entirely unpleasant, but added that despite their youth and relative inexperience the Girls wouldn't be pushed around. They knew what they wanted.

The girls then took a leaf out of Take That's book by choosing a specific showcase through which word of mouth could start. Their choice to launch 'Wannabe' on its

incredible success was The Box, cable television's own version of MTV, which differs from its most famous relation in one important respect: like a video jukebox, it plays viewers' requests. The Box was first to screen a Spice Girls clip, weeks before their debut single actually hit the shops, and the response was an avalanche of votes.

The Spices responded to this outpouring of enthusiasm by filming a video introduction to the members of the band – an expanded version of their 'Wannabe' rap, if you like – and viewing figures went through the roof. And anyone in a cabled-up area who wasn't plugged in soon found a good excuse for visiting their neighbours!

The rest of the UK got a look-in as the girls travelled the country on a three-month tour of local radio stations. As well as giving them the chance to reprise their acappella

antics, they made sure those stations would be waiting for their first release to pop through the letterbox with bated breath. And if they wanted some station identification jingles done at the same time, no problem! Then came a tour up and down the coastal resorts with the Radio 1 roadshow, spreading the word about five zany girls with a different image and a distinctive sound.

Top Of The Pops was the next target, of course – and in a matter of months the five Spices would become such regulars on the programme that when it won the Best Young Persons' Programme award in the National TV Awards, guess who went up to collect the trophy? But their first TOTP appearance was anything but in the flesh as, by chance, they were on a Japanese tour when the single hit the top. Maybe no-one had expected it to succeed so quickly…

However, with characteristic panache, they turned a potential crisis into an unforgettable piece of TV by performing a live satellite link-up from the sacred Naritasan Temple. In 36° heat and dripping humidity, they took 16 takes to achieve perfection – but it still looked fresh and fun. And by keeping the party-style video under wraps for another week, they established a momentum that would bring them seven consecutive weeks at the top – quite a feat for an unknown act's first record. The Wannabes were about to make it, and make it **BIG...**

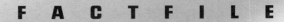
FULL NAME: Geri Estelle Halliwell

DATE OF BIRTH: 6th August 1972

STAR SIGN: Leo

PLACE OF BIRTH: Watford

HEIGHT: 5 ft 2 ins

EYES: Blue

DISTINGUISHING MARKS:
Tummy button pierced, hot pants in all weathers and red hair

WHAT DOES IT TAKE TO MAKE A SPICE GIRL?
Geri says you can be mad as long as there's method in your madness

IN A PREVIOUS LIFE:
Geri was a TV presenter on Turkish TV, a club dancer in Majorca, an aerobics instructor, a barmaid, cleaner, model...

SPICY SURPRISE:
It was those nude modelling shots, until the Papers got hold of the story

WHAT THE OTHER SPICES SAY ABOUT HER:
She gets everyone's name wrong, can be very naughty, and is totally independent

WHAT HER MUM THINKS ABOUT THE SPICE GIRLS:
Geri says her mum wants her to get a proper job, have a nice boyfriend, and settle down...

GERI

GERI SAYS SHE'S THE "BOSSY" ONE OF THE GROUP

FIRST CONTACT WITH THE OTHER SPICES:
Struck up conversation with Victoria in a Tank Girl queue

STATED AMBITION:
To own an Aston Martin DB6

GERI'S PERFECT MAN SHOULD BE:
A good snogger, very attentive, charming, androgynous

DECLARED HUNK IS:
Noel Gallagher

Geri calls herself the bossy one, and it's true that although all the Spice Girls are equal, Geri is a little more equal than the others. The eldest of the five, and unafraid of saying exactly what she thinks, she's really the undisputed leader of the gang who originally came up with the name for the group. Her red hair is perfect for a fiery Leo, a husky spokeswoman for Girl Power. Her clothes style has a Seventies edge, her attitude is full-on Nineties, and if you don't like it, keep it to yourself: one thing she hates is narrow-mindedness. If you do meet her though, you won't be short of conversation, since Geri reckons she can and will talk to anyone... She's got a lot to say! Independent and adventurous, she's been getting plenty of attention from the tabloids, but she'll ignore that. Anyone who says they flash at people 'just for fun' can't have too many hang-ups. In any case, she's probably hard at work practising the Spice Girls dance routines. It's the kind of grit and determination that backs up her ambition: Geri says she admires the Iron Lady Maggie Thatcher, but would also like to be reborn as Mother Theresa, a bank robber or a queen!

ON SPICINESS

Geri's recipe for success: the fact that all the Spices sing, all of them dance, and all of them write their songs. In short, they're the ones who are calling all the shots.

ON BEING TOGETHER

Considering the amount of time they spend together, the five Girls get on remarkably well, says Geri, allowing them to stay friends but be perfectionists as well.

ON FIRST IMPRESSIONS

Geri thinks that when people first come across the Spice Girls in person, they realise straightaway that they aren't a bunch of airheads, because they control what goes on. If other people can't handle it, well, that's their problem.

ON THE MUSIC BIZ

One of the problems, according to Geri, is that if you're a woman in the music industry, you have to make your voice heard as powerfully as possible or else people just think you're stupid. So they either think you're a loudmouth or a wimp.

ON GLOBAL AMBITION

Geri's declared aim is for as many people as possible to share in and enjoy the Spice Girls' adventure. And to bring that adventure to all the corners of the globe.

ON HOW TO COPE WITH DEPRESSION

If you're ever depressed, Geri jokes that the Spice Girls' solution is to take off all their clothes, and then do a streak down the nearest hotel corridor!

MEL C ON GERI

One of Geri's attributes, says Mel C, is the ability to change her image at will. And she likes to dress up - apparently she turned up for work once wearing a nightie.

ON TAKE THAT

Geri loved the band, and hopes that Mark Owen finds success, to prove wrong all those people who think he's a "bimbo" with a nice smile. She says she'd happily eat him for breakfast!

ON WHAT THE WORLD NEEDS NOW

The time is ripe for some strong females, says this rebel who definitely does have a cause. It's time to get up and shout.

ON GIRL POWER

The philosophy behind Girl Power wasn't something the Spice Girls just dreamt up. Geri thinks that they actually tapped into the way that girls feel right now.

"I read once that

your personality is

like a muscle.

You have to use it."

"We do things in a tongue-

in-cheek way. We are a

bit fruity, a bit spicy, but

we have fun with it."

GERI ESTELLE HALLIWELL

When the Spice Girls' first single was released, 'Wannabe' entered the UK charts at Number 3 on 20 July and, just one week later, deposed teen king Gary Barlow from the Number 1 slot. The girls, still in Tokyo, celebrated in fine style, Mel B drinking from two bottles of £120 a throw champagne at once and demanding a fat cigar as she partied with the others at a karaoke bar with cocktails on tap.

It wasn't the first time champagne had come into the Spice Girls' life – Victoria, who rarely indulges in alcohol, had been persuaded by her friends in the group to imbibe the famous 'rock'n'roll mouthwash' after their contract with Virgin was signed. The evening provided great frivolity for all concerned and plenty of fodder for a music press hungry for news of their night out.

There was even more to celebrate, now: not only had the Spice Girls become the first female group to top the charts since the Bangles' 'Eternal Flame' seven years earlier in 1989, but they were also the first all-girl British group ever to reach Number 1. And before anyone gets too smart, Bananarama were partly Irish!

Sales records continued to fall like ninepins. By the end of July 'Wannabe' had been certified gold (400,000 sales) after only two weeks on the chart. The third week at Number 1 saw them

overcome yet another challenge from the ashes of Take That – Robbie Williams' debut single, 'Freedom' – while their fourth week at Number 1 saw 145,000 copies sold in a week, three times more than Los Del Rio's 'Macarena' at Number 2, securing them a platinum disk for 600,000 sales.

Their fifth week at the top allowed them to rack up a further 125,000 sales, nearly twice as many as 3T at Number 2, while the next week saw them see off George Michael's 'Spinning The Wheel' with 110,000 copies as opposed to his 90,000. 'Wannabe' had now sold nearly 850,000 in Britain alone!

The champagne corks were popping in Virgin's office after week seven when 'Wannabe' equalled Meat Loaf's 'I'd Do Anything For Love (But I Won't Do That)' as the longest-running Number 1 in the label's 23-year history. Sales were now nearing

the million mark, and the latest challenger – Kula Shaker's 'Hey Dude' – still lagged 25,000 behind the Spices' nifty 900,000 sales.

All good things have to come to an end though, and 'Wannabe' finally conceded the top spot in mid-September, dropping to Number 3 behind Peter Andre ('Flava') and the Fugees ('Ready Or Not'). But even this was cause for celebration as a weekly sale of 75,000 took it over the million mark – only the third single to top a million in 1996 after Babylon Zoo's 'Spaceman' and the Fugees' 'Killing Me Softly'.

That wasn't the end of the story, needless to say, and as 'Wannabe' was released worldwide it topped the charts in no fewer than 22 countries! Most asked question about the catchiest song around was what exactly 'zigazig ha' was…the nearest to a sensible answer seemed to be that it was their own nonsense name for a cigar!

One confirmed non-smoker is Sporty Spice (Mel C), who plays for a ladies' football team in Hertfordshire. Though promotional commitments meant she spent a lot of the 1996-97
season on the road rather than on the pitch, the good news was that

Virgin Records paid a four-figure sum in sponsorship to get their name on the front of the shirts. So maybe Mel might give her beloved Liverpool strip a rest one of these days…

FULL NAME: Melanie Jayne Chisholm

DATE OF BIRTH: 12th January 1976

STAR SIGN: Capricorn

PLACE OF BIRTH: Widnes, near Liverpool

HEIGHT: 5 ft 6 ins

EYES: Hazel

DISTINGUISHING MARKS:
Celtic band tattoo on right arm and an inexhaustible supply of tracksuits

WHAT DOES IT TAKE TO MAKE A SPICE GIRL?
Mel C says it's being into Girl Power and not taking any crap from lads

IN A PREVIOUS LIFE: She did sessions as a singer, some ballet dancing, and worked in a chip shop - and almost made it into the cast of Cats

SPICY SURPRISE:
Mel C says she and the others wanted to do a moonie on Top of The Pops, but it was banned

MEL C'S PERFECT MAN SHOULD BE:
A good laugh, who can get on with her friends, and who, not surprisingly, is into footie

DECLARED HUNK IS:
Bruce Willis

WHAT THE OTHER SPICES SAY ABOUT HER:
She's diplomatic, not bossy, so she helps sort things out for the band

WHAT HER MUM THINKS ABOUT THE SPICE GIRLS:
Mel C says her mum was in a band herself (and her stepdad played in a Liverpool band too) so she's really understanding

MELANIE C

FIRST CONTACT WITH THE OTHER SPICE GIRLS:
Did a dance show with Mel B

STATED AMBITION:
To be an excellent footballer (she'd love to be a striker for Liverpool) and to see Liverpool win the Premiership, FA Cup and Coca-Cola Cup in one season

MUSICAL TASTES:
Bruce Willis, Madonna, Neneh Cherry

If Victoria is the lady in the Spice Girl's line-up, then it's fair to say that Mel C is the ladette (as Mel B puts it) of the band. Sport is a major part of this athletic Liverpudlian's life. She's a keep-fit enthusiast, who doesn't smoke. She's a talented gymnast who's known for her backflips. She loves to chat about football, particularly Liverpool Football Club. And she plays whenever she can for a women's football team. She and Mel B fight from time to time (Geri has to intervene and usually gets on the receiving end for her pains!), but she's not really as pugnacious as she might seem. The discipline she brings to her sport and her lifestyle means that she is effectively the minder of the band. She's tough and pragmatic, and claims she's not really interested in romance, but she is always helping the others out, like a protective tomboy of a sister, keeping them away from the kind of rude, narrow-minded people she doesn't like. So does this sports mad, highly focussed individual have any weaknesses at all? Well, maybe just the one: Chinese food...

ON ATTITUDE

Says Mel C, it doesn't matter if you're a bit of a big mouth. The Spices don't mind as long as you've got a fresh attitude. After all, every day could be your last, so go for it!

ON RESPONSIBILITY

Because the Spice Girls do everything they do themselves, they have to have what Mel C calls "conviction". They don't have, and don't want, the luxury of blaming decisions and choices on somebody else.

ON FRIENDSHIP

When Mel C was at school, she remembers that there was a lot of bitchiness around. But now she's noticed that it's disappeared within her friendships, and she puts that down to the confidence to be honest with each other.

GERI ON MELANIE C

One of Mel C's characteristics, according to Geri, is that she looks after people, for example carrying your suitcase if it's a bit on the heavy side.

A nice person, but tough and determined with it.

ON SELF PRIDE

The times they are a-changing. Mel C's rallying cry is that girls should be loud, and they should be proud. They should be ultra-confident, and tell lads either to get their act together or get lost.

ON FRIENDSHIP

Mel C sets great store by friendship. Like Mel B, she believes that when it comes to the crunch a good friendship is better than a boyfriend, because it will never end.

ON GIRL POWER

Feminism has become something of a misused and abused word in Mel C's view. Girl Power is the 1990s version. If women band together and show a united front, that solidarity creates the power.

ON FAME

Mel C, as everyone probably knows is a major Liverpool fan. The best side-effect of the Spice Girls' fame, she says, is that they let her into Anfield for free now!

ON KEEPING CONTROL

When they started out, the Spice Girls were managing themselves, which set the tone for their career. That control over their lives is something Mel C is determined to hang on to.

AS A TEENAGER

When Mel was 15 or so, she remembers modelling herself on Neneh Cherry. Permed hair, large dungarees, Reeboks and a dollar sign dangling round her neck.

"A bloke's best chat-up

line with me would

be an invitation to a

football match. I'm

not really interested

in restaurants and

romance and all

that."

MELANIE JAYNE CHISHOLM

With the world-wide success of Wannabe still humming from continent to continent, the buzz now was for the next Spice Girls single – could it be anywhere near as good, or as successful? The girls' record label, Virgin, weren't taking any chances, bringing forward the release of the Chemical Brothers' 'Setting Son', a collaboration with Noel Gallagher from Oasis and another surefire hit, to avoid a bottleneck at the top. And sure enough 'Say You'll Be There' was Virgin's highest recorded 'ship-out' with 334,000 on order by the week before release. It sold 350,000 in its first week in the shops, and was certified platinum in October.

Again, the video for the single was a significant factor in catching public attention. Unlike the party-style 'Wannabe', the scene switched to an outdoor setting in the American desert, with Madonna's ex Tony Ward as one of the supporting cast. Cool choreography, even more extravagant costumes and some weird and wonderful frisbee-type weapons all played a part, too, while the male of the species ends up thoroughly put in his place… blindfolded, if our eyes didn't deceive us, by a black bra!

Significantly, it was 'Words' from the inheritors of Take That's boy band mantle, those Dublin charmers Boyzone, who Girl Power knocked off the top when 'Say You'll Be There' entered the chart at Number 1. It then kept East 17 and Gabrielle's 'If You Ever' at bay in its second week

before falling to Robson and Jerome's 'What Becomes Of The Broken-hearted'.

But the Spice Girls didn't have broken hearts… not a bit of it! Their second hit still registered an amazing 1,735 radio plays in a week. And with a follow-up – 'Two Becomes One', their plea for safer sex – already the bookies' favourite to be the Christmas Number 1 over the usual all-star competition, no wonder they were smiling ear to ear.

Early November brought the release of 'Spice', their first album, which few people realised had been in the works for months! It had already gone silver (60,000 sales) before release, and despite heavyweight competition from the Beautiful South, Simply Red and the Beatles came straight in at Number 1.

With its outstanding songs like the 1970s disco-flavoured 'Who Do You Think You Are', the extra-funky 'Something Kinda Funny' and the pure pop of 'Love Thing' on board, there was no doubt that each and every track had hit single potential.

After November had seen them land the plum job of switching on the Christmas lights in London's Oxford Street – an honour few showbiz veterans ever aspire to - December found them headlining the televised Smash Hits Poll Winners Party. Then, after a quick jaunt round Europe recording TV spots for their new single, it would be off to the States for three months. What was the betting Bill Clinton would be offering to play a little sax with them? Their first full-scale British tour with band was scheduled for later on in 1997 – an event they were all looking forward to.

And if the hits ever did dry up, they could always pick up an offer from the Fantasy cable TV channel, who had allegedly offered them £1 million to strip off in front of their cameras. In your dreams, guys… but knowing the Spice Girls there's every chance they'd de-bag the camera crew instead! That's Girl Power – and in the gender revolution, the Spice Girls were already guaranteed to be Number 1 with a bullet.

FULL NAME: Emma Lee Bunton

DATE OF BIRTH: 21st January 1978

STAR SIGN: Aquarius

PLACE OF BIRTH: Finchley, North London

HEIGHT: 5 ft 2 ins

EYES: Baby blue

DISTINGUISHING MARKS:
No tattoos or body piercings, but she's pretty unmistakable

WHAT DOES IT TAKE TO MAKE A SPICE GIRL?
Emma says it's being strong and determined and having fun

IN A PREVIOUS LIFE:
She was a dancer, singer, actress (appeared in The Bill once), before joining the Spice Girls straight from school

EMMA

FIRST CONTACT WITH THE OTHER SPICES:
Victoria, who was in a musical with Emma when both of them were young

STATED AMBITION: Wants everyone to enjoy the Spice Girls music

MUSICAL TASTES:
Garage, house

SPICY SURPRISE: Told *Smash Hits* she wears leather underwear!

EMMA'S PERFECT MAN SHOULD BE:
Naughty, a bit cheeky, has to make her laugh. A good body, well cut. But ginger-haired lads are a no-no.

DECLARED HUNK IS:
Johnny Depp, also George Clooney

WHAT THE OTHER SPICES SAY ABOUT HER:
She doesn't look naughty but she is, she's always there for cuddles, and she adds a human touch to everything they do

EMMA SAYS SHE'S THE "BABY" OF THE GROUP

WHAT HER MUM THINKS ABOUT THE SPICE GIRLS:
Emma says initially she thought it was a religious cult!

Even if you didn't know for sure, you could hazard a guess that Emma was the youngest Spice Girl. A penchant for baby pink or blue clothes, anything furry, fluffy, shiny or lacy, topped off by a very cute face. It's not surprising that she's universally known as the Baby of the group, the sugar bringing a dose of sweetness to the spiciness around her. She likes a nap, and has been known to doze off pretty well anywhere. She likes to hug and show plenty of warmth and friendship. She lives with her mum, who's like a flatmate and has a poster of the Chippendales up on her wall. One of Emma's biggest fears is loneliness. This is a Girl who likes to give and receive bags of affection, not to mention bags of sweets! Since she announced to the world in an interview that her weakness was for doughnuts, she's become a single-handed promoter for the confectionery business. So how does she manage to keep a figure that is trim, slim and shows not an ounce of spare fat? The rest of us can only watch and marvel. But don't be completely fooled by the cute image she puts across. The other Spices say that although she has a totally innocent face, and can smile and dimple her way through anything, like a cream eclair she's nice... but very naughty. Could be she's the wickedest of them all!

ON STREAKING DOWN A CORRIDOR

One of the wildest things Emma recalls ever doing. The Girls were feeling like they, well, just wanted to go wild. Off came everything, and they ran, screaming, down the corridor.

ON A CELEBRITY LIFESTYLE

Emma says they don't go to many parties on the showbiz circuit, because it's not really their kind of scene.

ON GOING SOLO

The simple answer is that Emma wouldn't. She's got four of her closest pals for company, that's why she loves being in the band. Sharing time and having a bit of a laugh with her best mates.

ON BOYFRIENDS

Because Emma's mum always told her that nobody was good enough for her, she learnt how to be strong and stand up for her rights.

ON BOY BANDS

Emma reckons it's tough for some of the boy bands that have been, let's face it, manufactured. If they don't get to know what's going on or why decisions are being made, it's as hard as the actual work.

MEL B ON EMMA

She can get away "with murder", as Mel B puts it, like a little kid who is really really naughty and then charms you with a kiss.

ON CRACKING THE MUSIC BIZ

The five Spices set up a showcase performance for music publishers, with money that their parents stumped up. Emma remembers that after the show, they coolly waited to see who'd put up the best offer.

ON DAY TO DAY LIFE

Emma says that with the Spice Girls, what you see is exactly what you get. So if you happen to be lucky enough to come across them shopping at the supermarket, they're just completely themselves.

ON THE SPICE GIRLS SECRET

An intriguing comparison that Emma makes is that the Spices are like The Simpsons show. Both of them work on two different levels.

ON THE BRITS

Emma tells a story that Ulrika Johnson was looking stunning at the awards. Emma flashed her a smile, but didn't get one back, so when she walked past she cheekily pinched Ulrika's bum!

"My nickname's Angelica

the Rugrat 'cos I always

wear my hair in bunches.

I'm a Londoner and I love

the smell of candyfloss."

EMMA LEE BUNTON

All Action
Nick Tansley : 5, 6, 7, 8, 9, 10 (top), 14 (inset), 20, 21, 23 (top), 24, 26, 27, 30, 32, 33, 34 (top), 36, 37, 39, 42, 44, 45, 47, 48, 49, 54, 56, 57, 60, 61, 63
Suzan Moore: 10 (bottom), 25 (left), 28, 34 (bottom), 50, 52, 58
SKI: 23 (both)
Dave Hogan: 18 (far left)
Davies/Peters: 43 (right)
Ellis O'Brien: 64

LFI
David Fisher: 1, 2, 11 (main), 19, 22, 38, 46
Andy Phillips: 14, 16, 40, 62
Colin Mason: 31
Redferns
Brigitte Engl: 11 (inset), 13, 25 (right), 35, 59
Barbara Steinwehe: 55 (both)
Rex
Richard Young: 18 (second left)
Julian Makey: 29
Jonathan Buckmaster: 43 (left)

The Publisher would like to thank the following publications for their permission to use quotes in the book: p.15(top) Smash Hits, p.15 (bottom) The Face; p.27 Live & Kicking Magazine, BBC Worldwide Limited 1996; p.39 (top) Smash Hits, p.39 (bottom) Time Out Magazine; p.51 Time Out Magazine; p.63 Live & Kicking Magazine, BBC Worldwide Limited 1996